NOT SO DIFFERENT

Armaan Vir Kumar

This book is dedicated to my favourite person in the world, my sister Nishtha. This book is for you and all the lessons you have taught me about resilience and never giving up. A special mention to mom and dad for being the best parents I could have ever asked for. The book is a testament to the lessons you have taught me and the love that binds us.

A big thanks to my mother for helping me write this book. It wouldn't have been possible without you Mom.

Contents

Now I Have to Share

Sunday 8:30 am, July 2012

I woke up, rubbing my eyes as the early morning sunshine crept into my room. I stretched my back as I got out of bed. I was excited as it was my dad's weekly off from work. It was that one day in the week when my dad spent time with us. No everlasting phone calls, no working on his desktop. He would dedicate the day to the family and of course that meant mostly to me! After the hugs and kisses from my mom, dad and I got down to business discussing the multiple options that lay with us to spend the day. We decided… why not start the day off with a quick game of football.

In response to my dad's pass, I shot the ball too hard, barely missing my mom's head by a whisker. "Phew… good save!" my mom exclaimed, "Armaan! Be careful! Is this how you are going to behave when the new baby comes to the house?" What? Did I hear that right? Baby? *Who's baby? When is it coming? Which floor would it live on? Where was it coming from? How was it coming?* Questions kept popping out of my head but did not reach my mouth. And then I decided to not lose my peace of mind to something that did not even exist - many larger and more critical issues had already occupied my head: how to beat my dad in the game of football. And most importantly, how do I become the top scorer in Subway Surfers?

December 2012

Life was more or less the same for the next few months. The only noticeable difference was my mom's stomach, which was just growing and had started looking like a balloon. Worried, I asked her what was up and that's when the "big news" was thrown at me. There was a baby in the stomach and the baby was coming from there to stay in our house! I had completely forgotten about the "baby"! Now that was A LOT to process and understand. Over numerous conversations with my parents I learned that it would not be an 'it' but a he or a she. The baby was going to be a real human being and would apparently play with me and talk to me - I was frankly quite confused but seeing the excitement on my parents' faces, I kind of got interested in the big change as well.

March 8th, 2013

The moment I woke up, I saw my dad hurriedly rushing around the house, asking me to get ready as soon as possible since he had a surprise guest waiting for me. After saying this, I realised he wasn't in the room anymore. I wore my navy blue T-shirt with a tiger printed on it with a pair of black trousers. I rushed out to see my dad booting up the car. The car ride was filled with many questions. I asked him, "Will the guest play with me? Is it that uncle who brings sweets? Oh, is it that aunty who talks a lot? Are my cousins surprising me from Dubai?" I still didn't know who we were going to meet! Soon enough, we parked near a hospital. That's when dad smiled at me and announced, "Armaan, the baby is here." Oh, the baby!

As we entered the hospital and I peered into the numerous rooms and cubicles; I saw many small babies. I wondered how the doctor remembers which baby belongs to which family. Whose baby goes where? What if they get mixed up? I realised it was my moment to be agile and watch out for a mix-up or if anything went wrong. Finally, we entered a room and there on the bed, I saw my mom, with many wires going in and out of her body. I immediately went and hugged her and asked her what the wires were for. "She needs them for energy Armaan," said my dad. "Can't she just eat food or drink something for that?" I asked. They both chuckled but my attention was drawn to a small tray on the other side of the room where my other family members had gathered. I went over and saw a small, pink, doll-like toy wrapped in a piece of white linen cloth. "When can I play with it, papa?" I asked. "Not it, Armaan, play with **her.**"

"She is your sister."

That's How Sisters Are

May 2013

Having zero experience of what living with a sister meant, I went back home with my "new family" ready to experience this adventure. Little did I know that I was entering a zone of invasion where that little doll wrapped in white cloth had descended with a secret mission to take over my world. Before I even knew it, she had crept into every space that I once was the sole owner of and without an invitation, established a central position. Be it school drop-offs in the morning where she would hang on to my mom like a kangaroo from the baby bjorn or night times when she would be stuck on my mom's lap when she read to me. She silently became a permanent fixture in all the special moments which I thought would always be mom and my exclusives.

Many familiar faces kept visiting our house unannounced. These were the same relatives who once called me cute and made peculiar sounds in appreciation of what I did. However, I began to realise that they were now using the exact same expressions for not me, but her! I remember my grandmother's sister looking at my sister, saying, "She looks exactly like her father!" C'mon! That was a serious lack of creativity. They said the same stuff to me a month ago! How can they switch sides so soon? How unfair was that? Surely these adults would have a larger vocabulary! The invader soon became the Earth and all satellites revolved around that tiny body. When she napped in the afternoon I could no longer play with all my cars and blocks as the sound would wake her up! At mealtimes, she became the chief guest, brought to the table with all eyes on her every move. She took over everything that was once mine: my pram, my bedroom, the steriliser and the hardest of all, my parents. The sad and worrying part was that there was nothing I could do to stop this invasion.

I slowly began to realise that the invader was there to stay; definitely not going away, leaving me with no option but to make peace with the changing circumstances. I learned perhaps my *first lesson in life: that if you cannot defeat the person in the front, befriend the person*. After all, there was nothing I could do but share my world with this new entrant in our lives. Also, somewhere in the deep corner of my heart I started finding the new entrant "cute" and interesting. As the days dragged on, I started getting more and more used to her strange and sometimes endearing antics. Sometimes, I actually enjoyed her being around. Especially when she started growing and cooing making adorable, funny sounds. I loved it when she would hear my voice and kick her hands and feet in excitement and then try to grab my finger or hair, whatever she could get her hands on. The invader soon became a part of my little world.

As time went on, she stopped talking the little that she did, and her cries got even louder than before. At times, she would start shaking weirdly, as if something had taken control of her body. My friends told me their sisters were the same.

August 2013

As the months went by and my sister started growing, she became way more vocal. She started making more noises and would convey her intentions through different sounds of various frequencies. At times, I used to get super annoyed, especially when she would be in a cranky and fussy mood, constantly crying until she got what she wanted. The sound would be one which never ended and would constantly get on everybody's nerves. I remember that once, she wanted her red toy that made loud sounds of 'Old Mac Donald' when one touched it. She cried and flung her arms and head and miraculously, everyone understood exactly what she wanted through these antics! Not only she got what she wanted, no one reprimanded her for bad behaviour!

Sometimes, I would really feel the urge to talk to someone about the matter at hand. However, I could not go to my parents, for obvious reasons. Smitten by her cuteness, they always seemed too spellbound to utter a word to her. Instead, I decided to consult some of my friends. I told my best friend Nitish, about how annoying it was at times. I told him every last detail, from when it would start to where it would end. He too, had a sister just like me. She was just a few years older than us.

"Can you believe it?" Nitish said, his eyes wide with surprise. "Our sisters are exactly the same."

"How so?" I asked, intrigued.

He chuckled, shaking his head. "Whenever my mom refuses to give her something, she starts crying. And she won't stop until she gets what she wants."

At first, I was puzzled by this. But the more we talked about it, the more it made sense.

Nitish nodded, his expression growing serious. "We should ask Akaash too. He's got a sister, and you know how strong he is."

"That's a great idea," I agreed. "Maybe he's got some tips for us."

So, we went to see Akaash. Despite his tough exterior, he said that he was facing the same challenges. "It's like living in hell sometimes," he confessed, looking a bit defeated.

Hearing this, I felt a strange sense of relief. *It's not just me, then. It's several of us going through the same thing.* I guess that's just how sisters are!

Distancing Differences

September 2013

As things started settling down, I realised one day that my sister had become a lot quieter than she had ever been.

I saw a growing tension in both my parents. I was only around 4 at the time, and my sister was about 6-7 months old. My parent's strained expressions became more frequent, a silent alarm that my 4 year old mind couldn't fully comprehend. Despite sensing something was off, I remained blissfully ignorant of the storm that lay ahead. The excitement of my new school, long playdates with my best friend and watching countless drag races were a big distraction. However, somewhere in the shadows of my beautiful world, I could not help notice both my parents devoting much more time to my sister. There was also a sudden surge in the number of times my parents started visiting different doctors with her.

The first real shock came to me when one night, while I was getting ready to go to bed, I saw my mom sitting on the white sofa in our living room, crying. I was extremely shocked. For me my parents were superhumans who could do anything. Never once did I expect either of them to cry, especially my mom. My heart sank for one of the first times in my life after seeing her cry. She saw me and immediately started wiping her tears to try and hide it from me. I went over to her and tried to comfort her to the best of my abilities. She kept telling me to go and sleep as I had school the next day but I refused to go until she told me what was happening. After much persuasion, she told me that my sister was going to be very sick. Well, that was not a problem at all! I explained to her that people fall sick all the time and that there was no need to be so worried as medicine could easily cure her sickness. "Yeah, Armaan. I know, I shouldn't be so worried." was all that she told me. I went to bed shortly after, thinking that everything was sorted out and the next morning my family which included my new sister would be a happy normal family again. Things happen. Kids get sick and things go back to normal.

November 2013

With every passing week, I noticed that look of concern and tension growing at an exponential rate on both my parents' faces. My only source of information on what was happening was constantly observing my mother's expressions. I was glued to her face each time I saw her speak to anyone - to my father, to her best friend who had started frequenting our house a lot, to her spiritual guide. Though she thought she was doing a great job of hiding her feelings from me, I was observing her too closely. Little did she realise that her face was not only the most comforting factor for my little brain but also the window through which I viewed the world outside. Their worried expressions were making me uncomfortable and uprooted. I just had to know what was going on. Trying to solve this big mystery, I could pinpoint that it was definitely something to do with my sister and her antics – after all, her arrival had displaced me as well. But I had dealt with it by speaking with my friends who had sisters and had found my own path to make peace with her. I thought it would be a great time to *share my new observations and learnings with them.* I had prepared an entire speech, ready to convince them that there was nothing to be worried about and that it was simply the way all sisters were. Little did I know that my parents had their own speech prepared for me.

By this point, my sister had stopped making the sounds she used to and had started making new, higher-pitched sounds. She also started doing weird movements with her hands which my parents termed as "stimming." Stimming is self-stimulatory behaviour which manifests as repetitive movements such as rocking back and forth, repeated vocalisations, etc. While many of us stim in some way or the other it is often associated with kids who have neurodevelopmental conditions.

Even though I was only 4, my parents maintained transparency with me, never hiding the facts from me. They explained to me that my little sister had a problem in her brain that made her act slightly different from others. The problem was big and would interfere in many aspects of her growth and development. There was no medication that could be given to cure her and she would need a lot of help from us throughout her life. I heard and understood what they were trying to tell me but it did not make much of a difference to me. At the end of the day, to me, she was only my sister whom I loved and cared for the most in this world. She was my sister, and I would do anything for her, no matter what.

December 2013

I still remember that my tiny brain and body went through a roller coaster of emotions which has taken many years for me to be able to pen down. On one side I found nothing wrong with her, and on the other side, I saw my parents run pillar to post with her, trying to understand and find the right solution. Sometimes they took me along, sometimes they organised play dates and other times they left me with my grandparents. I too, seeing my surroundings began to feel stressed. I kept on probing many people with as many questions as I could in order to try and get some information out of them. Each time, it was only my parents who shared all the information with me in detail. Thinking that they were burdening me with a bit too much, they tried to keep me distracted. Apart from normal school hours, they enrolled me in various after-school activities such as football, and chess. A little later, they introduced me to drums. I began to play football at the age of 4. At first, I never really enjoyed it, but as I grew up, I developed a great love for the game. A similar story took place with chess except that I enjoyed the game straight away.

Even though I was grateful for all the distractions they provided for me, my heart and soul were with them. Mom and dad were a BIG part of me and seeing them in distress upset me. Seeing my little baby sister having to go through so much was also far from comforting. I saw my cousin sisters, and I saw the sisters my friends had, and honestly, I never saw an issue; in my head, that's how sisters were. At the same time, my mom made me read a book which I will never forget called: *My Naughty Little Sister*. And trust me, I saw NOTHING wrong. For me, my sister had come into my life, and that's the way she was, the way sisters were.

Latitude, Longitudes and Lessons

Lesson 1: *Getting into a routine*

December 2013

In the months that followed, I became accustomed to the newness in my life. I had started "BIG" school which began at the same time that my sister was born and oh man, they were both massive changes in my peaceful little life. I made some great friends at school, and I would really look forward to meeting them every day. I especially looked forward to my school drop-offs and pick-up times when my mom showed up every single day, no matter what. In my very stressful situation, at that point, her face brought a sense of calmness to me.

There was a little routine that included the fact that my parents would need to take my sister to doctors. In my little world, that had become a part of our life.

Lesson 2: *There's more to the world than just my country*

Around Diwali of 2013, I could tell that something was out of order. My parents looked exceptionally occupied. I saw my mother spend hours on the computer doing something, and I could hear hushed discussions between my parents. Though she thought she was doing a great job hiding how she felt, I could tell that my mom looked more worried than ever—I just knew that she was not the carefree smiling mom I had known once. And then things changed.

"Guess what?" Mom said one day in December. There was a twinkle in her eyes as we sat down for dinner. "We're going to London!"

"London? Really?" I nearly jumped out of my seat. My mind raced. I thought of snow and Santa Claus on the streets, Christmas trees! and even Thomas the Tank Engine and Postman Pat!

I clapped my hands, my imagination already racing. *Oh man, this is going to be amazing!*

But what came next confused me a little. My mom's face turned sombre. She looked softly into my eyes and said that this was not a holiday; we were going to "fix my sister." Ok, wow, that changed the image in my head a little. But after a bit, I felt even better. Images of my sister being "fixed", my carefree parents and me playing with snow and meeting Santa came back and life looked all well. And this became the introduction to a whole new chapter in my life. A chapter that continues to date and has come to occupy an integral part of all our lives. Our trips to London have almost turned into a ritual now, and we have learned to find rainbows among the clouds. It also became the teacher that taught me many lessons that I still hold dear.

Although I knew about the existence of places outside my tiny little world, I had never experienced them fully and realised that it was a whole different world out there. People have diverse lifestyles and I found it interesting how people in different places went about their lives.

We reached London, and one of my mom's friends was there to pick us up at the airport. And we had a LOT of luggage. My parents had told me that we would be gone for a while. And so we reached our apartment, which became our home for the next 4 months. The smell of the air, the roads, the streets, and everything else were so different from back home. The one thing that I found the strangest was that the sun went down at 2 pm and it would become night! How strange was that? I looked for Santa from the minute we landed but did not find him.

Lesson 3: ***Teamwork and assigning responsibilities***

I would wake up every morning, watching my mom cook, something I never saw her do in India as we always had help back home. She would cook and clean the apartment and then take my sister for some tests to the hospital. We hadn't met the doctor yet as my sister first needed to go through several investigations. My parents split their responsibilities: my mom would take my sister to the hospital and my dad would take me to see the city, the National Museum, the Palace, Winter Wonderland and whatnot. I loved that. Those moments when I got to spend time with my father are still dear to me. The best part was the London buses! I was fascinated by them, and every day I would ask my dad to take me on a new bus to a different route. These tiny moments of fun and bonding really got us closer as a family and some of the memories from these trips are etched in all our hearts. They never fail to bring a smile to our faces.

This is where I learned my 3rd lesson: that one needs to work as a team when faced with challenging times. In hindsight, and through a more mature lens that I wear today, I feel it was my parents' strong love and respect for each other that they did what they did. My sister went through all her investigations and they ensured that I was not left out and got to experience the city and learn from its vast history. At the end of the day, we would all gather as one family in the apartment that had now become home. This was also the time that Nishtha was rechristened several times by me – "Piggy", "Bubs the Tubs", "Digs the Pigs, the famous", and whatnot! But "Piggy" clearly won the competition.

I still remember how Mom and Dad would clear up the kitchen while I played with a rattle with Nishtha. Then the 4 of us would watch *Diners, Drive-ins and Dives*. Nishtha, of course, would not understand but get excited with the screen. Mom and Dad took turns cooking, cleaning the kitchen and feeding us. Yes, I was all of 4 and needed some support to eat the complicated meals.

Finally, the day arrived when we went to the Great Ormond Street Hospital(GOSH) to meet the doctor. My 4-year-old brain was working again, and my imagination was running wild trying to imagine what the doctor would look like. There had to be something different and special about this doctor for my parents to have come all the way to meet her. I had a picture of a large lady with lots of muscles, big glasses and large eyes, carrying lots of medical equipment with her.

The first appointment is etched very vividly in my brain. The waiting areas in GOSH have lots of play stations. Being a children's hospital, these stations provide the children while waiting to meet the doctors an opportunity to play and also a place for parents to leave the siblings. I found it really cool. I remember sitting there colouring with my mother waiting to see the doctor and mustering up the courage to ask her, "Mom, what is wrong with, Piggy?" "Armaan, there is something wrong in her brain, and we also do not know exactly what, which is why we have come to meet this doctor." My mother, trying to hide her nervousness, replied through her smiling eyes. But she was my mom, and I could always tell when she was hiding stories from me. And just then, I had a revelation! I got it! Just a few months ago there were these strange bugs which had entered our house causing a lot of unrest. The mission was to kill them instantly else they would cause havoc! And that is when I had heard of termites. That's it. Termites!

"Mom, does Nishtha have termites inside her brain?" and that is when I saw my mother laugh in her old carefree way for the first time! "No, Armaan she does not have termites! I wish it was that though, but no, it is something else." I felt silly for having come up with such a crazy explanation, yet seeing my mother laugh like that seemed worth it.

And that's when the doctor called us—that was my other lesson: ***Expectation and reality can be two very different things.*** Much against the image I had painted of her, the doctor was a petite, humble lady who carried no medical equipment on her and had the loveliest smile. My mother's friend had accompanied us, volunteering to babysit me while my parents went in to see the doctor, but they insisted on keeping me with them.

We sat there for a time that appeared like an eternity. I could not understand what the doctor said, but from the way my parents looked and exchanged glances, I knew that it was not good. There was something heavy and stiff in the room and I did not like the feeling of it. On the ride back home, there was silence. I remember seeing my parents hold hands, each looking out of the window of the car. When we reached the apartment, I was too tired. I ate a yummy meal that my dad got and slept. But in my heart, I knew that something was wrong. Something happened that broke my parents that night.

A few days later, Mom and I sat in a cosy corner of a pizzeria, the aroma of freshly baked pepperoni and mushroom pizza filling the air. My mom gently took my hands across the table, her eyes filled with love, meeting mine.

"Honey, I need to tell you something important about your sister," she began, her voice soft yet steady. "There's something wrong with her brain. It's something that needs a lot of treatment and medicine."

I nodded, squeezing her hands, the warm pizza momentarily forgotten.

"We're going to stay in London for a while, until a big part of her treatment is done," she said. I was okay with that; I loved London—the bus trips, the adventures, and how we all spent time together in the evenings.

I smiled, thinking of those bus rides and evenings.

Her eyes shimmered with unshed tears as she added, "But, sweetheart, your sister... she's not going to be like other kids."

Sadness washed over me, not just for my sister but for my mom too, seeing her so upset. But in my heart, nothing changed about how I felt for my sister. "I love her, Mom. She's perfect to me. Just the way she is."

Mom smiled, a tear rolling down her cheek as she reached for a slice of pizza to hand to me. "Thank you, my dear. That means more than you know."

From then on, London became an important part of our lives. Every year we go to see Piggy's doctor for her tests and medical reviews. We continue to have some traditions: the first meal we order in when we land, the last meal in the same restaurant after meeting with the consultant, and the walks in the parks.

London was the beginning of my experiences and travelling to see the world. My mother did not stop. While medically, she had found the right choice in London, she continued to look for opportunities to equip my sister with her development. The medical condition had caused a lot of damage to her brain and she needed lots of help. That took Team Nishtha to many places, including Philadelphia and Toronto. The places were different, the people were different, and the cultures were different. But in those differences lay our routines of staying in an apartment, going grocery shopping and looking for Indian vegetables as my sister was on a very strict nutrition programme which required my mom to cook for her. My mother cooked, dad cleaned and we tried to slowly add mini vacations and sightseeing into these trips. They continued to split duties, places where my sister couldn't go, one of them stayed with her and the other took me. I was always grateful to them. In all these places, they ensured that I never missed out on sightseeing. Though secretly, I longed for the 4 of us to do everything together and not have to split up, but that became the norm for a bit.

A couple of years into making these trips, my best friend from India moved to London. On one hand, having the absence of my best friend at school was extremely saddening but on the bright side, I would have something extremely fun to do on the trips to London. Despite the distance between the 2 of us, not a year has gone by where we have not met each other.

Lesson 4: **Eat, Pray, Love**

This inevitable and precious part of my life showed me the power of love, the power of hope and the power of faith. In spite of getting the worst prognosis for my sister, my parents did not give up. They challenged everything that was told that my sister would not be able to do - everything, bit by bit. *It taught me the lesson of never giving up, even when everything stood against you. It taught me the value of relationships; real relationships were those who stood by you when nothing was on your side.*

My best friend and his family have been instrumental in my sister being where she is. It was his mother who helped us find the doctor in London. And the neurologist was the reason why my sister is where she is today. In spite of not being related to us by blood, the way they supported us and continue to do so is difficult to encapsulate in words. As fate would have it, after the first few years of us going to London to meet the doctor, he and his family relocated there. My heart broke when they moved, especially since his house had become an extension of mine. Each time my mother anticipated a long day with my sister, I was shipped to Aryaveer's house. And his house always felt like home to me. His parents were always so welcoming. His move broke me, and I felt lonelier than ever. But the good part was that each time we went to London, I had a family there. Despite the distances, he and I have always shared a strong bond. Each summer, when we meet, we pick up like we never left, and I am grateful for this bond in my life.

My mother's 2 closest friends -from helping her pack for London to speaking to her on the phone to wiping her tears to taking turns to babysit my sister and me- were always there. As we have grown up, the nature of their interactions with my sister and me have changed, but they continue to remain an integral part of our lives. These people have stood beside us no matter what. They came whenever we needed help, even without asking them to. They've become a part of our family, and they are some people that I can be sure I'll never forget.

It has taught me the power of trust and true friendship, and knowing and understanding those people who'll stand by you no matter the cost and those that'll leave you in an instant whenever you go down. Today, these lessons have proven to be some of the most valuable I've ever learned and it helps me get through many tough times.

As a teenager, while I traverse the complicated path of social relationships, it can be very stressful and awkward for most children my age; Many times, the relationships that I have seen in very difficult times with my family have become my reference point. There is a big difference between people who will pretend to be there for you and people who will actually have your back. In my eyes, I am able to have 1-2 such friends in my life, which I do, for which, I feel fortunate and grateful.

Getting Close at the Time of Social Distancing

December 2019

My sister was consistently improving in various fields of her life. It was a lot of hard work. Nishtha's improvement had become the singular mission for my mother. She did not stop researching and reading about different strategies to improve her in different aspects. Many times, I would watch mom and fear that she was going to drive herself crazy.

Nishtha had challenges across all platforms: motor issues were a problem, cognition was an issue, sensory integration and balance were also issues. There was not one area that was not impaired. That made the task for my mother tougher. She researched on new approaches, conventional approaches and made sure that Nishtha received everything that would give her a fighting chance to march ahead. It was difficult seeing my mother so stretched and constantly pushing herself to improve Nishtha. I could sense the frustration in her sometimes, especially when she had been working for very long to develop a skill and there would be minimal improvement.

But despite everything that was going on in that part of her world, my mother always made a point to ensure that my needs were met as well and that I never felt neglected.

I was now in 5th Grade. Having been told that this would be my last junior year,' I had as much fun as possible. It was the year that I made a few close friends in school. I enjoyed being the senior boy in junior school. However, as the end of the year neared, news of a deadly virus traversing the globe at a never-before-seen speed was all over the TV and the papers. It was called COVID-19. I heard that it had started in China and was spreading to other parts of the world like the flu. There was no cure for this and the virus in itself being extremely contagious made it a force to be reckoned with. At this time, thankfully, no cases had been reported in India and life went on as normal for another month or so.

March 2020

As the cases were on the rise, increasing rapidly throughout the world, the Indian government too declared a complete country lockdown. People all over the country were forced to stay at home and work through the online medium. I had to attend my school online due to this very reason.

During the 2 years that we were in lockdown, there was hardly much to do. People could not leave their homes and school was online. I got extremely bored. Apart from playing online games with my friends for an hour or so a day, there was nothing much to keep me entertained. This boredom also led me to spend a lot more with my family and my sister. It was for the very first time where we got a lot of time to hang out with each other. We would play different games together and even though they were the silliest games imaginable, the fun we both had was out of this world. These were some of the best moments I've ever had with my sister. This time of being together has gotten us closer as siblings and we both know that both of us will stand up for the other no matter what. While everyone was distancing themselves from one another, my sister and I got closer than ever before.

I also began taking an interest in religiously supporting my parents in their journey to help make my sister better. My dad and I started cooking a lot of food during the pandemic, and it helped us both discover a side of us we never knew we had. We would watch tutorials on the internet and implement them into our recipes; it was great fun to be doing these activities with someone as close as your father. It was also during this time that I started choosing the clothes I wore, instead of getting help from my parents. I dove into the depths of my cupboard, exploring the unknown and found so many amazing pieces of clothes that I never knew I owned. I found a wide variety of colours and realised that there was a whole world of variety apart from my monotonous blue, black and grey. I started to understand my sister's problems more and gradually learned how to help her. I understood her daily routine from the minute she woke up to the minute she went to bed. I saw her struggles, put myself in her place and wondered how it would feel.

And then the inevitable happened. Both my parents tested positive for COVID. My father had already tested positive and had been isolated. Those were the early days of the pandemic when isolation lasted for 14 days. On dad's 12th day of isolation, my mother also tested positive and locked herself in a separate room. That left me and my sister outside with her nanny. I was in charge of managing her. Still nonverbal, she could not express how she was feeling as she did not see both my parents around. And so she did the next best thing she knew: she cried and cried till my ears hurt. How was I supposed to manage someone who would not stop crying? Then I had a brainwave. Mom and dad were locked inside for the next 2 days, and until my dad came out, I needed to tide through. Hence, I gave her an extra iPad! That brought a big smile to her face. So we both took our iPad and entertained ourselves. It made her calmer and more willing to reason with me. I also monitored her meals, her naps and her medication. For those 2 days, I became the bridge between my parents and Nishtha. When my dad came out, I was relieved! That was a huge responsibility on my shoulders and I was happy to pass the mantle back to someone else. And more than that, I was happy to have my dad back. I jumped up and hugged him, and we both ate our favourite meal, butter chicken, together.

Friends Indeed

The one big blessing I have had is that I have been able to make some great friends who have been a big support system for me. I was never the boisterous, outgoing personality and so, I never really had an army of friends. The friends I have made over the years have been few but they are the ones with whom I share an extremely strong bond.

I shared about my best friend in London in the earlier chapters. Thanks to the advent of the online gaming world, he and I manage to sneak a few hours every weekend to play a few games. And then I have made a really close bond with another friend. He is also, incidentally, my mother's closest friend's son and we both hit it off from a very young age. Being at mom's best friend's house, I got to spend many long days there as well – mom's way of ensuring that I did not lose out on what other kids my age did only because her hands were full. He and I became extremely close. The pandemic saw him migrate to Singapore. That was another big blow for me; I felt abandoned. 2 friends whom I got extremely close to both left. That is when this brought home a very important lesson for me – *it does not matter how many times one talks to a friend or how many play dates one has; what matters is the connection and bond that transcends all barriers.* Through all the years we have stayed in touch, and with both of my best friends who moved countries, I never feel that I am meeting them after a long time. Despite the different cultural experiences both my closest friends and I have gone through during our growing up years, we have only grown closer. They've always understood my sister's condition and will always provide their unwavering support whenever my family needs it. Even their families are always there for us, providing us with a place to stay when we visit their countries, helping us with things such as travelling to places in their city and most importantly being an emotional pillar for my parents. Their support is something to be truly grateful for.

However, I also experienced the other extremes of social networking, especially in school.

"Look who's here! It's the guy with autism in his family!" "Autism runs in your genes." These are some of the things I got to hear on many days when I went to school. It hurt me, yes, it still does, but there really isn't much I can do about it. Initially, I hurt, I cried and felt beaten down. However, with a lot of mindful and conscious practice of the 5X5 rule, (only worrying about something if it'll still matter in 5 days or worrying about people who will be important to me in 5 years.) I have learned to deal with these incidents better.

I've learned to bounce these feelings off and move on with my day because none of those people are going to matter 5 years later in my life. It was a turmoil for me; I love my sister and felt the need to do what I could to help her be comfortable. And yet such words, especially during the years when a lot of us try to fit in, threw me into a whirlwind of emotions. I wanted to stand up for my family and yet fit in with the larger "crowd." Was it hard? Yes, it was. It was hard and heartbreaking but I have learned to deal with this as I have realised the value of true and strong bonds.

Hearing such things as a child, I grew up to be a lot more sensitive towards others, and so did my close friends. I've always wondered if these people who tease you have even learned what sensitivity is. To this day, I fail to understand how those around me never went through the same. Some of my closest friends have always been with me and have never judged my sister or me due to her condition. These are the people who really matter in life - those who will stand by you no matter what.

My best friend in school has been friends with me for as long as I can remember and always stands by me no matter what. I fondly remember this one time when I was getting bullied for having a sister *'like her'*, and he seemed to appear out of thin air like a knight in shining armour and rescued me with his worded weapons and stood by me like a rock. I couldn't be more grateful for having people like him in my life, and I would do the same for him whenever he needed it.

It's a lesson I have learned perhaps a lot earlier in life. And it is something I would love to share with someone my age: ***it is not the quantity but the quality of relationships that sees one through. It is not about fitting into a larger crowd that does not understand and stand up for you but about having those 1 or 2 friends who will have your back no matter what.*** As a teenager, these are not easy realisations to have, and I have had my own journey in accepting and coming to peace with these facts - but now that I am here, I feel a lot more sure of myself and take pride in who I am. Once you are able to cross the bridge and come to terms with yourself, you are a lot more at peace with yourself.

More Than 4

They say it takes a village to get past an issue, and there is a great deal of truth in that. We have had an army of friends and some family who have stood by us during the toughest moments. We, as a family of 4, struggled to cope with the ever-challenging circumstances. Our other family members came to our help through some of our difficulties.

I think I have been fortunate enough to grow up with grandparents around. They bring another kind of joy and semblance into one's life. My maternal grandfather, I remember, accompanied my parents to most doctor appointments in the initial years. I could see him stand up with them like a rock. Later, after a few years, when I had grown up, I learned that he also went independently to several doctors with my sister's reports to understand if we were on the right path. He became one of my closest friend, confidant and coach. And he has always stepped in to have a little "man-to-man" talk, helping me stay grounded and feel loved.

My maternal grandmother tried to take care of me as much as she could, from playing silly games with me to spending hours playing Monopoly and Ludo with me to getting my favourite things to eat. She was a bundle of positive energy that I continue to look forward to. She has found her way to my heart through food and researching the newest flavours of ice cream—even today she always has a new flavour when I see her.

Similarly, my paternal grandmother was there to help and support us whenever we needed it. From accompanying me to my drums class to dropping me off and picking me up from play dates, playing a game of UNO and cooking the yummiest meals, she was always there. She inundated my mother with different mantras and forms of worship that she should perform, which, of course, my mother instantly turned down, but that was her way of helping.

While I know that my grandparents stood rock solid with my parents and continue to do so, the love that I got from them made me feel whole and complete.

My mother's sister has also played an integral role in helping our family tide through this time. Always the stronger and more stern one, she has ensured that we do what we need to at the practical level. She lives in Dubai, and visiting Dubai became another annual holiday destination for us. When we were younger, she would take care of my sister when we travelled there and gave us some time to explore the city. She, too, continues to push my parents to keep researching for more things that are possible. More than that, I think she manages my mother's mental health. In the initial years, when Nishtha was still getting better, my cousins in Dubai became my reference point on what a relationship between siblings meant. They looked after me, fought with me, chided me and loved me. Today, when Nishtha is better, I share the same equation with her.

In the early years, when I was shipped to friends' houses, I never realised that it was being done more to protect me, as my mother was going to spend most of the day taking Piggy to a hospital or so. Not wanting me to be alone, my play dates were organised to keep me distracted and happy.

They say that some family you are born with and some you make along the way; my mother's best friend clearly proves this right. In spite of having a very demanding career and a young child of her own to look after, she was a permanent fixture in our house from the time I can remember. When my mother got busy in hospitals or therapy centres, she took me over to her house. Her son and I are best friends, and I could never complain. She continues to be the emotional support for my mother, researches new approaches that can help her, and, I guess, is the only person in front of whom I feel my mother lets her guard down. Hence, now, when she visits us, after my hugs and polite exchanges, I let them be. Plus, both of them spending time together means I get unadulterated gaming time with no one to check on me.

These are just a few of the lovely people who have supported us in our journey. Like this we have had several people who came in and just became family. The nannies that have come to support my parents with my sister are just amazing. The sincerity and love I see in them is really adorable. Though I have to admit that they spoil her rotten and treat her no less than the queen. When the season of *The Crown* aired, I really could draw parallels between the way the Queen was woken up and how my sister is woken up! But I have seen them cry with my mother on days that were tough and celebrate every success of Piggy.

There have been a few people who also did not support us the way we needed, but as my mother always has said, **when we spend time focussing on doors that have been closed we fail to see the many doors that are opening for us**. So yes, people and help have always poured in for my sister, for me and for my parents many times from sources that we least expected. And it is that love and support that has enveloped us enabling us to grow and thrive with each other.

Armaan in Action

As the COVID pandemic seemed to be going on forever and ever, my role in helping my sister in her overall development got larger than before. With boredom taking over my world, I realised that one of the most productive things I could do with my time was to help my parents and my sister. Thankfully, I enjoyed it a lot as well.

To be honest, when the whole world shut down, another world opened up for me inside the confines of my own home. With school, extracurricular classes, play dates, etc. having come to a halt, I was home all the time. This was when I came to witness the life my mother and sister led every single day. I realised how my mother had intelligently structured my sister and my routines to ensure that when I was away at school or at my extracurricular classes, she dedicated 100 percent to working with my sister, and all the times I was home, I was made to feel like I was the priority. With the outings gone, I was always there, and my sister was always there, meaning I stood witness to everything that was going on.

For some strange reason, for the first time, I started feeling a sense of resentment for the amount of time Nishtha was getting from my mother. For the first time, I started feeling that maybe I was not the priority and that by being well and normal, I had probably done something wrong. Maybe if there was something wrong with me, I, too, would get that time and attention. For the first time, I craved that undivided attention and care. Maybe it was my boredom, maybe it was just staying home, or maybe it was my changing body and hormones. When it got to me, I decided to speak about it to my mother and that one conversation made me contextualise and normalise how I felt.

She got more time from my mother as she had A LOT of issues. Imagine not being able to communicate what one wanted, imagine not having a single friend to play with, imagine where every small activity that we did was a task, and THAT is why she needed more help. And then I realised during that conversation that in spite of that, my needs were also equally taken care of; be it me calling friends over, be it my studies, be it getting support from my parents, even for my extracurriculars like drums and chess, they never backed away. And for the first time during that conversation, I saw how tired my mother looked. Though she smiled warmly at me, I could see the years of exhaustion and pain behind them. She and Dad loved me a lot, and there was never a doubt about that.

That conversation was my metamorphosis into becoming the big responsible brother. I realised that I needed to play my role actively where I could. I needed to understand how to manage my sister better, as I loved her and wanted to help her. I wanted to see her improve. And that's when things changed. Though I was always an integral part of Team Nishtha, I took on a more active role. It started with small things like me taking over to play with her so that my mother could drink her coffee. I soon realised that games I wanted to play with her she did not like or maybe found difficult. And so I learned what she wanted to do and played what and how she wanted to.

Slowly, it transformed into bigger roles, like pushing her to speak so that she could become more verbal. I started visiting her centres when I could understand what children like her went through. I interacted with a few other kids who were fond of my sister. I also helped in taking videos of my sister doing various exercises (this part I hated and continue to do), which had to be sent to her therapists.

And the biggest of them all, I learned what needed to be done when she had a seizure. Though I was a passive witness to it for so many years, waking up in the middle of the night each time my mother was nursing my sister's seizures, I started playing an active role in timing them, ensuring that she was being made to lie in the right position. Cut to today, my parents can leave her with help who has even the basic training at home as they are fully confident that I know the protocol to be followed. And seeing my parents lay that trust in me and step out to find a few moments for themselves has been the biggest victory for me. One of my favourite times with her is when my parents step out for the night. First, we play a game where I act like a monster and chase her around the house. Her way of running and laughing when doing this makes my day. After that, we read some books together, and I show her my favourite football players as well. *Match Annual* is one of her favourite books, and playing football is one of her favourite sports! And if there is a cricket game that day, it becomes our match night. After that, putting her to bed and saying goodnight to her is the icing on the cake. As she has grown older, she has also started giving me my space. Now, she is comfortable and happy just reading a book and sitting in the same room while I enjoy an online game with my friends. When she wants to call it a night, she lets me know, and I make sure she is put to bed.

Beyond the confines of my home, my life too was picking up and how. There was lots to study, projects that needed to be completed and friends to catch up with. My friend circle continued to remain small, mostly because I found myself resonating with the few that were really my tribe. The sneering and passing comments about my sister continued, but with each passing year, I learned not to let it affect me. And that was my personal evolution. I began to understand who the real people were and who would always have my back and found avenues to explore that built my confidence back. Was it an overnight transition? No. It was many years of experiences, conversations with people who mattered, heart-to-hearts with my parents, and the love that I got from them, including my sister, that fuelled this change.

With every passing year, I find myself growing closer to my sister. Recently, after nearly a decade of being on a strict nutritional programme where she was not allowed to eat a lot of stuff, her diet has been allowed to be normalised. After tasting blood, she did not relent in stepping back from eating foods that were a big NO. Be it the packet of spicy chips or that last piece in the bowl of butter chicken, we fight over it and yes, I fight with her for that last piece- partly because that is what would transpire between any 2 siblings and partly because I want her to be able to fight for what she really wants.

Like Brother Like Sister

As I continue to grow, so does she. And with the passing years, I realise that I never noticed how she always looked up to me. She would try her best to copy me in any way she could. From checking what I was doing when she had to study, to starting to read football yearly Annuals, to watching YouTube videos of people cooking Chinese meals, to loving butter chicken; the list goes on and on. I can clearly see how she tries to be like me in many ways. And that's when I realised that she is Not so Different.

I have always loved irritating my mother; let's face it, it is a domestic activity that we all enjoy or have enjoyed at some point. And I am super proud of the fact that my sister has followed in my footsteps to the T. There are moments where I know she is deliberately testing the last drop of mom's patience, and then we exchange glances and she smiles at me; that exchange means the world to me. And those instances make me realise that in spite of all the issues that she has and all the labels she has been given, she is an ordinary 11-year-old, trying to live the best she can. She is what any other younger sister would be. That's how sisters are.

The most endearing thing is when my mother sometimes loses her cool with me; Nishtha's expression is one that visibly expresses how she doesn't appreciate the way I am being treated. In that moment, we feel united like one, where I feel that this stranger who walked into my life and tossed it over is my tribe and part of my army.

Despite the fact that she may have a million labels on her because of her condition, that there are many theories about her future, to me, she is just a normal sibling with the same traits as any other sister.

The one thing that motivates my parents, and especially my mother, to keep at what she is doing, is to ensure that my sister will be able to live life independently. It's one of her biggest fears: who will take care of my sister when she's gone? In my head, that is a baseless fear. As long as I am around, I will watch out for her, not because it is my responsibility or that is what is expected of me, but because I love her dearly and see it no other way.

I have always tried to reassure my mother that I will take care of her, but she refuses to allow that. However, each day is a small step in the long marathon ahead of us, and every bit of it counts.

Over the years, my love and care for Nishtha have only grown more and more, and I am willing to do whatever is needed for her whenever it is needed. Although I know I can't expect the same from her, it still doesn't stop me from trying my best to be there for her when she needs it. For her, we are her world. She doesn't have any friends, so I always try to be understanding and friendly with her so that she has someone like that in her life, someone who's not always telling her to get off the phone or to sit down to study.

My sister and I share many memories together, and I hope she looks back on them with as much joy as I do. Just playing with her and watching her smile and laugh makes my day more than anything. She seems to know exactly what goes on in my mind and always tries her best to tell me that she knows. From helping her get up the slides on the playground to watching her do it herself a few years later, is just one special moment out of many. I could go on writing for hours on end about the endless experiences we've been through as siblings. I really couldn't ask for a better sibling than her.

When I started cycling, she was my biggest cheerleader, and today, I am her interim trainer. When we get into the pool, I am her lifeguard, and when she is tired and wants to get out, she spots me in all the dozen heads in the pool and asks me to help her out. When we fight over the last piece of butter chicken in the bowl, or for that last French fry or when we cut each other in a game of Ludo, it just feels like a bond that is ever so precious; that's how much she is like me.

Up until now, she has never been able to tie me a rakhi due to her motor issues (a sacred thread that a sister ties to her brother) and that, for some strange reason, becomes a thing of tension among the extended family that gathers around on such occasions. To me, that thread is a thread; what we share with each other is far more deep and meaningful. A thread that she ties on me once a year has no meaning in front of the deep love and respect we share for each other.

She came into my life like an intruder but became an integral part of it as my friend, my confidant, my cheerleader, and my biggest teacher. Yes, Nishtha has taught me lessons in life that I would have never learned. ***She has taught me to stand up for myself, to understand what selfless love means, what fighting back with all one's might and what humility means.*** And she made me travel to places in the world that I would never have had if it was not for her!

Abnormal Community

Over the course of the last decade, the 4 of us have formed a team. One that has rules, values, mandates and time outs too. Howling, hurting, healing we have found our happiness.

What I give maximum credit to is that my mom really works hard in order to make it all feel normal for us. From morning to night, she works tirelessly to help my sister and take her to therapy sessions and different classes. She ensures that we go out for meals, celebrate all occasions and do everything that happens in any family. While my mom is at home and helping my sister and me, my dad works every day at work and helps pay for all the bills and classes we go to. When he returns home, he's a completely changed man. He forgets about all the stresses of work and plays with my sister and me, never failing to make us laugh.

As a family, it has been a long and tough journey, but even today, we still fight with the same spirit we did all those years ago. It's a dream for all of us to see her better one day- a day where she can talk and do everything like her peer group. We've done so many things together - family building activities to be the friends in her life, travelling around the globe to different countries and continents to make her explore the world around us, playing weird games with her which she enjoys and can never stop giggling or laughing. The list is endless. This experience has taught us many lessons along the way, especially me at such a young age.

I've come to see and believe that families with similar conditions and challenges to ours love to connect and talk to one another and share valuable insights and lessons they learned along their journey. As a teenage boy myself, I never had the opportunity to talk to others and share my learnings and inhibitions. To feel there was nothing unusual at times, all it takes is one more unusual companion. I used to always think- is it only me, or is there someone else out there who is just like me? Well, I never really got an answer. However, I do think there is a need to have a platform where young boys and girls growing up with *Not So Different* siblings can connect, exchange how they feel, and work out strategies to help them and their siblings cope with their situation much better.

Setting up a forum for young kids like me who also have a sibling with a similar condition is my dream project. Through this forum, I want to connect numerous children who seek to understand the situation in a much simpler way so that they can also do their best to help out their families when they need it and at the same time, find the emotional strength to deal with days which may be hard and challenging. It also becomes a space where the siblings find an emotional connection, as it is hard to grow up in a situation where there is always a fire to fight. This idea is different from other forums as many of them are for the parents to understand the condition in much more depth and familiarise themselves with the lives they will have to take up. With the approval of the parents, I strongly believe that a medium like this, will help siblings like me, to navigate circumstances that can be demanding at times. It is in finding the understanding, empathy and support, that siblings like me feel that our situation is after all "Not So Different."

I also feel that as siblings to neurodivergent children, we need to be the mouthpiece and advocates to help build a world where these children are given equal opportunities - opportunities to study, travel, play, grow and live.

They may seem different, act different but they are not so different; they are ordinary children longing for love, acceptance and real friendships.